Unleash Your Business

A Step-By-Step Guide
To
Finding Financing
For Marketing
Your Home-Based Business

2012 EDITION

Dennis Lively

Unleash Your Business

A Step-By-Step Guide
To
Finding Financing for
Marketing Your Home-Based
Business

2012 Edition

By
Dennis Lively

Published By:
The LiveMark Company

No income claims are made or inferred in this work. I don't know what your skills are, or your work ethic, or your market, or anything else I'd need to know to even make an educated guess at your results. The contents of this book are my opinions and observations, based on my own experience, and should not be taken as anything more than that.

Nothing in this product should be construed as legal or other professional advice. If you need such advice, seek the assistance of an appropriate licensed professional in the relevant field.

Some of the things discussed in this book may involve activities which are regulated in various jurisdictions. You are responsible for complying with the laws where you live and where you conduct business.

You are solely responsible for the consequences of your use of this material.

2012 Edition Published by: Louden Digital & Print Publishing.

PRINTED IN THE UNITED STATES OF AMERICA DISTRIBUTED WORLDWIDE.

Table of Contents

Foreword

Before we even get started, we need to get some things straight. First of all, I am <u>not</u> promising you that I will get your business <u>any</u> form of loan or financing. That being said, this book <u>will</u> give you all of the tools and knowledge you will need to go out and get your own financing for your own business.

Secondly, I am NOT a lawyer or an accountant. The advice I give you is based upon 25+ years of being in business for myself. Always check things out with an accountant or lawyer if you have ANY doubts.

Thirdly, and most importantly, this book was written to enable you to get "MONEY TO MARKET YOUR BUSINESS" from the United States Small Business Administration, if you are a U.S. citizen OR, if your are a citizen of another country, a program similar to the SBA. There are many programs throughout the world that are set up along the guidelines of the SBA; some of them are even sponsored by the United States Government. This book will probably <u>not</u> help you if you intend to walk into a typical bank and come out with a loan for your business. My book will help you get started, but you will need more a sophisticated business plan than this book can cover. If this is what you want to do, I recommend "Business Plan Pro" by Palo Alto Software. The program turns out an excellent business plan, but requires a <u>lot</u> more work from you. You can check their software out by going to:

http://www.palo-alto.com/index.cfm

Specifically, the whole strategy behind this book is to give you the best chance of getting a business loan through the SBA. Why the SBA? Well, for one thing, lower interest rates. With the SBA guaranteeing your loan, banks look at you as less of a risk...therefore, lower rates. For another, the SBA has a TON of resources that will help you become a better businessperson; a more profitable businessperson. The agency has many dedicated employees who are eager to help you. By going through the process outlined in this book, you will allow them to process your application more quickly. This gets you YOUR money quicker...and allows the SBA personnel to spend more time helping you develop and prosper your business.

Home-based businesses are finally being recognized as an integral part of the world's economy. Financial institutions, corporations and even governments have slowly come to offer a degree of help for home entrepreneurs, like us. Admittedly, this help is sparse and not very easy to get, but it is getting better out there. The SBA is your most important doorway to receiving help in growing your business.

If you are a citizen of a country other than the United States, don't despair! Your country probably has a program like this. The fact is, almost every country does and they are woefully underused. The same procedures asked of someone planning to apply to the SBA also apply to you. You actually have some advantages. Most likely, the programs in your country are just setting there waiting for applicants. Even more likely is the fact that they are not used to seeing business plans as well thought out and well structured as you will develop using my book.

In a general sense, this book will make you take a good close look at your business; at what it costs to run it and at what you can reasonably expect to profit from it. It will lead you into making a marketing plan, with measurable, results-oriented goals. It will require that you know which marketing methods are the most cost-effective for YOUR business, and how they fit into YOUR marketing plan and more importantly, YOUR marketing budget. Most importantly, this book will help you put a value to your business...not only in dollars and cents, but in your mental value of how important it is to you.

The greatest by-product of this book for you, gentle reader, is that it will make you view your business as just that...a business...with written plans, budgets and, hopefully, profits. That does <u>not</u> mean that: it still can't be fun; it still can't be run in your spare time; it has to be a burden to you. By taking these few, painless, fun steps, you will view your business differently...as just that, a business, putting money in your pocket each month...a business that you know all about because you planned it all out. YOUR business will be YOURS indeed!

This is gonna be fun! You'll see!

Getting Started

Here's our Plan of Action over the next few chapters.

1. We will write down some information about your business,

2. We will get some facts and figures about your business together,

3. We will get some facts and figures about your industry together,

4. We will get some facts and figures about your advertising types together,

5. We will write a simple business plan,

6. We will write some simple budget projections,

7. We will write a simple marketing plan,

8. We will write a simple marketing budget,

9. We will write a simple loan request.

Facts and figures...business plans...budgets...loan requests...any idea what you're going to need to do this part? NO, not Tylenol or a stiff drink! Here's what you're going to need:

1. About 4 hours, uninterrupted, split up however you can put in that much
      time,
2. Some scratch paper,

3. A calculator,

That's about it! The next 4 hours will be the most important 4 hours you have ever spent on your business. It will make a huge difference, not just in money, but also in how you view your business. It will make you get excited about what an opportunity you have in your hands. It will make you start to see that, with planning and work, you can have your dreams...AND it will be down on paper...it will be in writing...it will take the first step to becoming a reality. Now that's exciting! Let's get started!

Let's Look At Your Business

The very first section of your business plan will be called "the Executive Summary". Sounds fancy, doesn't it? Actually, all it is, is a couple of paragraphs that summarize all of the other pages that follow in your business plan. The standard thinking is that busy executives will not take the time to read your entire report' so you have to summarize it for them. That's simply not true. They will read every word of it and check (and double-check) every one of your figures. Wouldn't you, if someone were asking you to lend them money?

This is what an "Executive Summary" looks like:

Executive Summary

ISP is in the rapidly growing field of Internet Access. We sell dial-up and DSL Internet Access to consumers throughout the United States. We purchase these services from our parent company, ISPVIP.

Our service is faster than our competitors; more full featured than our competitors and is less expensive.

The Internet Access market has grown by 5% the past year, which means over 1,000,000 new users were added in 2002. In addition, over 1,500,000 present users switched Internet Access Providers in 2002. Both of these facts make for a very large market of potential customers.

Historically, we have averaged new sales of $ 100.00 a month. However, since our customers stay on our service for an extended period of time, we have accumulated a monthly income of $1300.00 over the last 13 months.

Our costs of doing business have averaged $1000.00 a month over the last 13 months. This gave us a profit of $300.00 a month.

We want to develop our business through a targeted marketing plan which, we project, will increase our business by 100%since we have done no marketing to date.

The corresponding business growth will allow us to repay the funds loaned to us, continue our marketing efforts and make our business much more profitable.

We are asking for a $5000.00 loan, to be repaid over 5 years at an interest rate at or below 10%.

You really can't finish this page yet, unless you already know how much you make, how much it costs you, the statistics on your market, your marketing plan and costs, and how much you are going to request in the loan. So, you don't have anything to write right now. This is just to show you where we are going to end up. You can start to jot down ideas for this page if you want.

Your Business in a Nutshell

The next section of your business plan is entitled

"The Company Summary" and it does just that,

summarizes what your company is, what it does and how it

does it. Here's what a "Company Summary" looks like:

Company Summary

Founded in 1997 on a part-time basis, Occasions is a small business designed to meet the needs of the ever-changing social world. Portland, Oregon is the current home with plans to expand to branch offices within four years. Occasions' staff of two, with numerous contract vendors, plans events, writes event-planning products, and trains area students in the art of event planning. Occasions is invested in the community it resides in.

Occasions is, in part, the answer to demands of the social world, on the working family, heavily-burdened office, out-of-town business, or special occasion in need of special recognition. As a business, we understand the needs of public and private organizations. As parents and family members, we understand the needs of setting special time apart from other events in our lives. Occasions strives to accomplish these goals, in Portland and eventually other areas of the Pacific Northwest.

You CAN do this one now. Just write a couple of paragraphs along the same lines as the example above. This is where you can describe YOUR vision of the company, as it exists now. Describe why you formed it, in general terms.

Don't get carried away! Show your enthusiasm for the business here. Finish it up before you go on. It should take you, maybe 30 minutes. When you're done, set it over on the side of the table. <u>You are now about 8% done!</u>

Who Are You And What Do You Do?

The next section of your business plan is called "The Management Summary". This is the part where you tell them all about your qualifications, your experience, your talent...you get to brag a bit. Just make sure you can verify everything you say. You definitely don't want to be asked for a reference from one of your jobs and they never heard of you! Here's what a "Management Summary" looks like:

Management Summary

We are a small company owned and operated by Ralph and Mabel Smith, husband and wife, as a Subchapter S corporation. Ralph is the developer and designer of the products, and Mabel manages the office.

Ralph has 23 years of experience in widget design. He spent 13 years as a widget designer for XYZ Corp. before it was sold and another 10 years as Chief Widget Designer for ABC, Inc. He is still employed by them.

Mabel has 20 years experience as a bookkeeper with the local school district. She also keeps the family budget in line.

Management style reflects the participation of the owners. The company respects its community of co-workers and treats all workers well. We attempt to develop and nurture the company as community. We are not very hierarchical.

This one should only take you a few minutes. One of the things you need to know, or decide, is what legal structure your business has. The majority of small home businesses are categorized as sole proprietorships. In other words, not a corporation or partnership. If you have created a corporation, an L.L.C. or a partnership, just state that in your summary. You will need to have a copy of any incorporation papers for your business plan package.

Describe your experience in detail. If your home business is selling widgets, tell them how you got experience in selling widgets. Try to make your experiences fit your business whenever you can. If you have no direct experience relating to your business, explain how you got interested in the business and what research you did into the product/service you sell. If you have management or financial experience, highlight those jobs.

The whole idea here is to show the lending institutions that you know what you are talking about and have some experience to back it up.

You will need a copy of your resume' to add to your business plan. So, if you have one, get it out and put it with this page. If you don't, you can go to: http://www.10minuteresume.com/ to build yourself one in less than 10 minutes.

When you get that done, set it over on the pile you

started. <u>You're now about 16% finished.</u>

What Do You Sell?

Our next little project is "Services" OR "Products" OR "Services and Products". It depends on what you sell. This is just a list of your products/services, their prices and a brief description of each. If you sell TONS of products or services, just pick a representative few; DON'T list the entire catalog!

Here's what a representative "Services/Products"

would look like:

Services/Products

The Boulder Stop sells the entire raft of coffee drinks: lattes, mochas, cappuccino, espresso, and a delicious house blend. The coffee and espresso beans are freshly roasted by Espresso Harvest. Our team of two part-time high school students will create the beverages for customers. They will be trained in "The Art of Making the Proper Espresso Beverage" at Espresso Harvest, which hosts such classes once a month.

The Boulder Stop also sells carabineers, friends, nuts, ropes, webbing, shoes, and harnesses; our product mix is sufficient to satisfy even the most hard-core enthusiast. Below is a listing of some high-end products that we market:

- *Black Diamond Camelot Canning Device - $50 to $100*
- *Wild Country Forged Friends with Sling - $35 to $65*
- *Hugh Banner HMS Locking Carabineer - $12 to $17*
- *The North Face Bouldering Sweatshirt, Men's - $85 to $105*
- *Mammut Flash Duodess 10.5mm Dry Rope - $185 to $200*
- *Boreal Ace Rock Shoes - $150 to $170*

All products are quality checked when they arrive and quality checked before the customer takes them home.

This is just a list of products and special things you do for your customers. If you have any printed material about your products/services, put a copy of each in your pile over on the corner of the table.

This part of your plan should take you less than an hour. You know your products. You know which ones sell the most. Describe them. Put the prices there next to the description. Add any promotional materials you have and you are done!

Put this page over in the pile along with any of your printed promotional pages.

<u>You are almost 24% done now!</u>

It's time for a little break. Go get a Pepsi or something and stretch your legs. Up until now we have been just writing things down that you already know. We have just put that knowledge into a structured form that will make it easy to read and understand for the lenders. In the next sections, we will be doing some "figuring", so get your calculator and scratch pad ready. See you in a few minutes!

Where Do You Sell Your Gizmos

Okay! Ready to get started? This section is the first one in which we will have to generate some numbers. What we are trying to accomplish here is an in-depth look at the market your business operates in. If you sell widgets in 2 counties in Northern Wyoming, then that's your market. If you sell e-books to everyone in the United States, that's your market.

Here's a market analysis I did for a small business

I just became involved in:

1.Go to: http://www.census.gov/index.html and on the right side locate your state (West Virginia), click GO,

2. In the top left hand corner, find your county (Wetzel), click GO,

3. Scroll down to "households", write down this number. (7164)

4. You may want to do this for surrounding counties, too.

5. Take the number of households and multiply it by 52% (3725)
that's how many internet users are in your county, according to http://www.cyberatlas.com

6. Multiply this number by 80% (2980) That's how many dialup users are in your county

7. Go to http://www.aol.com http://www.msn.com http://www.netzero.com and http://www.earthlink.com and check to see if they have dialup numbers in your county.

8. My county has an earthlink dialup number.

9. Here's the percentage of the dialup market that each competitor has:
AOL.............27.5%
msn...........9.4%
netzero......5.6%
earthlink....5.5% again, these figures come from
http://www.cyberatlas.com

10. In my county's case earthlink has 164 subscribers

11. Here are the monthly prices for each competitor:
aol..........$23.90
msn........$21.95
netzero....$14.95 (customer service costs $1.95 a minute)
earthlink..$21.95

12. Next, check around and see what local ISPs are in your county...(I have 3.)

13. See what their prices are ($15.00, $19.95, $19.95)

14. See what features they offer (none of them has accelerator, spam control, popup control or parental control)

15. Even if all of the "big boys" are in your county, remember that AT LEAST 8% of these subscribers switched services in 2002...PLUS, look at the price differential !!!

16. Back to my home county, 2980 dialup users; none of the competitors have anything to compare to what I have to offer...THAT'S $2980.00 A MONTH FOR ME TO REACH OUT AND GET

17. MY SURROUNDING AREA HAS OVER 10 TIMES THAT MANY SUBSCRIBERS...THATS OVER $30,000.00 PER MONTH...NOW THAT'S EXCITING!!!!

Now, let's take a look in detail at what I did and how I did it. First of all, I got some census statistics from *http://www.census.gov/index.htm*. If you are selling nationwide, use the United States numbers. I used "households" because most households only have one Internet account. If you sell a product or service that is routinely 1 per household, do the same as I did. If you sell a product/service that every person in a household may buy, use the population figures.

If you are selling in a specific area, go to the "state" section and use that. If you need them, there are county figures and city figures as well. The main thing we have to get at is the number of how many potential customers are in your market area.

The next thing you need to do is find out how many people use your service or product. I was able to find my statistics at CyberAtlas. Com, a site dealing with Internet usage statistics. I found that site by using Google and typing in "Internet Statistics". If you sell widgets, try "Widget Statistics". The supplier of your widgets will probably have a lot of these statistics as well and will be glad to share them with you since you will be a bigger customer if you get more money for marketing!

Next, you need to find out where else you can buy your product/service in your market area. Who is selling them? What do they charge? Are their widgets different than yours? Is their customer service different than yours? Do they charge for shipping? You probably know a lot of this already, but it is important that you write it down.

If you tend to sell to a specific age group, you will notice that the census data is broken down into "below 5 years of age" and "18 years of age and under". You can extrapolate how many kids are between 5 and 18. You can also conservatively figure 50%-50% male/female, if you sell predominately to one gender over another. You get the idea...the figures are there...play around and get the statistics that apply to your market.

When you are talking with your supplier or researching on the Internet, try to find a ranking of your competitors and their market share %. It is probably there, if you dig a bit. Your suppliers won't give you specific numbers, but may give you a rough percentage that you can work with. Write these down.

If you are a citizen of a country other than the United States, all of this still applies to you. You just have to get your statistics from: http://www.cia.gov/cia/publications/factbook/index.html. Yep! That's right, the CIA. Don't worry, they don't monitor this site and it gives great information about almost any country in the world.

Do you see what we are doing here? We are giving concrete numbers and references to people who live for numbers and references. We are putting it in a form that is easy to read, yet gives the information fully. That's important!

On the next page, I've included a simple work sheet to help you put your statistics in a readable form. You can use this exact form in your business plan.

Market Analysis Work Sheet

My Market Area is:_____

There are _____ **households/people in this market area.**

____**% of these people are potential users of my product/service.**

OR

I market mainly to_____ **. (age group, gender)**

There are _____ **people in this market segment.**

____**% of this market segment are potential users of my product/service.**

My competitors are:

Name	Price	Difference from my product/service
_____	_____	_____
_____	_____	_____
_____	_____	_____
_____	_____	_____

My competitors' market share:

Name	% of market
_____	_____
_____	_____
_____	_____
_____	_____

References: _____, _____,

_____

    See what this work sheet has done? It has put a concrete face on your market. You can positively say that there are X number of potential users out there. You can positively say who your competitors are, what they charge and how your business is different (better?) than theirs. You can point to references to back up your numbers.

    You probably already knew, instinctively, what your market was. This just puts it in writing and proves it.

Your next step it to write a paragraph or two using these numbers like this:

My company sells Internet Access to consumers in Wetzel County, West Virginia. In this area there are 10 other Internet Access Providers. The market for Internet Access has grown an average of 5% each year for the last 3 years. There are 7618 Internet users in our county. 381 new users, on average, are available each year. 610 present users switched services last year.

My Internet Access Service is faster, more full-featured and less expensive than any of my competitors. I also am the only provider to offer free customer service, 24 hours a day, year-round.

My main competitors are: XYZ, who charges $ 23.95, ABC, who charges $21.95, DEF who charges $19.95 and GHI, who charges $14.95. Currently, XYZ has 25% of the market, ABC has 10% of the market, DEF has 7% of the market and GHI has 5%. My company currently has 3% of this market. The remaining 50% of the market is shared among several other smaller firms.

By increasing my market share to 8%, I can generate an additional $1500.00 per month in gross revenue.

See, the work sheet made that easy. Write your paragraphs. Add your worksheet to the pile over on the corner of the table and add your paragraph sheet to it when you are finished. Guess what! <u>You are 1/3 of the way done!</u>

What Have You Done Lately?

The next section of your business plan is very straightforward. It's called "The Historical Sales Data Sheet". This sheet does a couple of things: it shows your sales, on a monthly basis, for every month that you have been in business, and it will allow you to see the " ups and downs" your business goes through over a period of time. You know, maybe January is always a slow month for you and July is always busy. This sheet will verify that in writing. The cycles of YOUR business will be important when we come to projecting income later on in this book.

Here's what a "Historical Sales Data Sheet"

should look like:

Year	Month	Sales	# sold	%
2003	January	100.0	5	3.4
2003	February	180.00	9	6.2
2003	March	280.00	14	9.6
2003	April	220.00	11	7.6
2003	May	300.00	15	10.3
2003	June	200.00	10	6.8
2003	July	240.00	12	8.2
2003	August	260.00	13	8.9
2003	September	360.00	18	12.3
2003	October	200.00	10	6.8
2003	November	220.00	11	7.6
2003	December	360.00	18	12.3
Totals		2920.00	146	100.0

That's pretty self-explanatory. Start a new sheet

for each year you have been in business. If you have been

in business just a few months, use those months. If you

have been in business for over 3 years, limit your sheets to

just 3.

Do you see what these sheets have done? Again,

they have solidified your business into something down on

paper. Something you can prove. Something the lender can

work with. They have also shown you which months were

historically busy and which ones weren't.

When it comes time to project your income, you can use these percentages to vary your new monthly totals in a way that is historically correct for your business.

When you have finished, put all of your sheets over on that growing pile on the corner of the table. <u>You're just about half finished!</u>

What Did That Cost You?

The next section of your business plan is an important one. It is entitled the "Historical Costs Analysis". The first and most important thing you need to know is; HOW MUCH DOES IT COST TO RUN YOUR BUSINESS EVERY MONTH? This may seem obvious… "I use free advertising, I work in my spare time…it doesn't cost me anything to run my business." WRONG! At least, that's the wrong answer to give if you want to receive any kind of funding. "If it doesn't cost you anything and you still make a little bit of money every month, then why are you coming to me for extra funding? Just save up your profits until you have enough to mount a marketing campaign." That's exactly what the lending officer is thinking.   YOU NEED TO SHOW OPERATIONAL COSTS EACH MONTH!

Here's how to do that. If, for example, you made $200.00 dollars last month and your family income, not counting the business, that month was $1800.00; your total income was $2000.00, right? Your business accounted for 10% of the total. 200 divided by 2000. Doesn't it stand to reason that it accounted for at LEAST 5% of the costs? Corporations do this routinely…its called cost allocation.

Figure out your percentage of income by dividing the amount you make from your business by the amount you make from any jobs your household has. Take that number, in this case 10% and divide it by 2, just to be conservative. Write it down! You'll use it in just a bit.

Now, let's get to what it REALLY costs you to run your business. Here are some of the costs:

Direct Costs:

Wholesale Cost of Goods: If you buy a widget from the supplier for $8.00 and sell it for $20.00, you don't make $20.00; do you? You have to take out what you paid for the item. The $20.00 you received from the customer is Gross Profit; the $8.00 you paid for the item in the first place is your Cost of Goods; and the $12.00 that remains is your Net profit.

Cost of Sales: If you have to ship the item to the customer, that has to come out of the Net Profit. If you had to send your potential customers a flier to get them to buy, then the cost of the flier and the postage both have to come out of your Net Profit. Other examples of this category are:

*If you are on the Internet, the cost of your Internet service, or at least a portion of it;

*The cost of web hosting for your website;

*The cost of your domain name;

*Any cost that is directly due to your business.

<u>Allocated Costs</u>:
(Using our 5% example from above)

5% of the mortgage,

5% of the utilities,

5% of the house insurance.

Please note that these figures aren't for tax purposes…they are merely used as budget figures to arrive at a true cost of doing business.

So, let's start a list of your costs.   It will look something like this:

Type of Costs   *2003*
Cost of Goods   *$1168.00 (This is the amount you paid for products/services you sold)*
Advertising   *$ 438.00 (Self-explanatory)*
Shipping   *$ 379.60 (Cost of shipping either to you or your customer)*
Web Hosting   *$ 96.00 (Self-explanatory)*
Postage   *$ 192.00 (Self-explanatory)*
Mort. Allocation   *$ 300.00 (Calculated on 5% of a $500/month mortgage)*
Utilities Allocation   *$ 120.00 (Calculated on 5% of a $200/month utility bill)*
Insurance Alloc.   *$ 36.00 (Calculated on 5% of a $60/month insurance bill)*

Totals   *$2729.60*

Obviously, yours will be different. The main point

is that you need to be thorough and detailed in your

list. Explain how you arrive at allocations.

Now, let's take those costs we've just listed above

and turn them into percentages.

Costs	$ Amount	Units Sold	Costs/Unit	% Cost
Inventory	$1168.00	146	$ 8.00	40 %
Advertising	$438.00	146	$ 3.00	15 %
Shipping	$379.60	146	$ 2.60	13.5%
Web Hosting	$96.00	146	$ .66	3 %
Postage	$ 192.00	146	$1.32	6.5%
Mortgage	$ 300.00	146	$2.05	10 %
Utilities	$ 120.00	146	$ .82	4.5%
Insurance	$ 36.00	146	$ .25	1 %
Totals	$2729.60	146	$18.70	93.5%

What we've done here is to plug in the number of units you sold in 2003. That's the 146 in this example. I divided the Cost by the units sold to get a Cost per Unit. The percentage of Unit Cost is what your product/service retails for divided by the Cost per Unit.

$1168.00 / 146 = $8.00 (Your Cost per Unit)

$20.00 (Your Retail Cost) / $8.00 (Your Cost per Unit) = 40%

In other words, 40% of every sale that you made went to "Cost of Goods"...your supplier. 15% went to advertising...etc. You are left with a profit of $1.30, or 6.5%, on every sale you made.

This is an important sheet of paper, not only for your business plan, but also, for you, as a business owner. It shows the funding source that you are keeping accurate records of your sales (that's usually an easy one!) and your costs.

That's a step that the vast majority of home businesses never do. It immediately sets you apart and makes them start taking you a little more seriously.

It is also a great tool for you to see exactly where you money is going when it's not ending up in your pocket. In the example above, you would get a BIG heads-up if your shipping percentage came in as 25%! That would be a red flag for you to explore other, less expensive, ways of shipping.

See what I mean? This is a sheet you REALLY should do on a monthly basis, even if you never intend to get a business loan from anyone. It simply gives you more control over YOUR business.

<u>Well, you are WAY over half done now!</u> Put you Costs Sheets over on that famous corner and let's move on!

This is Where I'm Gonna Be

Those last few steps were a little difficult. The next one is a little more fun. This part of your business plan is called your "Sales Goals". It is just that. We will look at what you have done in the past and write down some goals for the future. Don't make the mistake of skipping this section. Goals are very important for a couple of reasons. Funding sources NEED to see them. They use goals to grow their own businesses and EXPECT you to have them as well.

The other, more important, reason is that nothing will happen consistently without goals being set and monitored on a routine basis. Have you ever used a "TO-DO LIST? If everything is written down in front of you, it is easy to go down through the list and get things done. Before you know it, the list is complete! Goals are just like that.

Any consistently successful businessperson will tell you that nothing really happened for them until they wrote down their goals and started working on the list.

Here's what a "Goals Sheet" should look like:

Goals For XYZ Company for 2004

1. I will increase my sales of widgets by 100% by December 31, 2004.
    A. This will be measured at quarterly intervals according to the following schedule:

1. Jan-Mar 2003 Sales = 28 units   Jan-Mar 2004 will = 56
2. Apr-June 2003 Sales = 36 units   Apr-June 2004 will = 72
3. July-Sept 2003 Sales = 43 units   July-Sept 2004 will = 86
4. Oct-Dec 2003 Sales = 39 units   Oct-Dec 2004 will = 78
5. 2003 Sales = 146 units   2004 Sales will = 292 units

2. I will decrease my Cost of Goods from 40% to 30% by December 31, 2004.
    A. This will be measured at quarterly intervals, as above.
3. I will decrease my Shipping costs from 13.5% to 10% by December 31, 2004.
    A. This will be measured at quarterly intervals, as above.

See how that's done? You have to decide what goals you have for the next year…do you want to increase sales? Use a very personal statement…I will…not we will or xyz will…<u>I will</u> increase my sales by X% by December 31, 2004. The company isn't increasing sales…we aren't increasing sales…YOU are!

You have to have a time limit on your goals or they are just words. When you say…by December 31, 2004, you are setting yourself a deadline, making a promise to yourself that you are much more apt to keep.

Finally, your goals have to be measurable. You can't just say, "I will make more money by December 31, 2004." How much more money? If you make 1 dollar more than last year, will you have really accomplished anything? Make it a number you can compare your last year's sales to. Did you notice I set up a schedule of when you are going to review your goals and put your target number right there where you can see it?

The next part of your "Goals Sheet" is an Action Plan. It looks like this:

Action Plan for Achieving my Goals

1. I will increase my sales as stated above by

  Implementing my marketing plan on a daily basis

  Providing excellent customer service

  Asking every customer for follow-up sales

2. I will decrease my Cost of Goods as stated above by

  negotiating with my current suppliers

  researching new suppliers

3. I will decrease my shipping costs as stated above by

  negotiating with my shippers

  negotiating with my suppliers for lower shipping costs

The Action Plan should be general at first and then, as you actually start to carry it out, become more detailed. "Negotiating with my current suppliers" would become "Call Joe Blow at ABC, Inc and ask for a better profit margin". At this point all you are doing is making a TO-DO List. Just go down the list, mark off tasks as they are finished, and you've started accomplishing your goals.

Your Goals and your Action Plan should both go on one sheet of paper. Don't get too wordy with your goals or plans. Make them short and sweet and to the point. Remember; make them personal, time-limited and measurable.

Goals can be very powerful for your future. Look at them often, change them as you need to, but USE them. For now, you can put this sheet of paper over on the corner of the table. See how that pile is growing? Time to take another break. When we come back, we'll be working on some marketing. See you in a few minutes.

My Marketing Plan

First of all, let me be very blunt!

I know what funding sources want in a marketing plan! They want to see proof that you have researched your marketing plan; they want to see circulation of newspapers, listeners of radio stations, visitors of websites…anything that will give them some NUMBERS to work with.

Your Marketing Plan is actually in 4 parts;

1. Your Marketing Strategy,

2. Your Marketing Research

3. Your Marketing Plan,

4. Your Marketing Budget

Your "Marketing Strategy" is actually only a few sentences long, but it is very important. It puts in writing exactly where you want to target your marketing towards.

If you already sell most of your widgets to males, do you want to increase sales to females? Or, do you want to target people 24-45 years of age? Only you can answer this one.   Put some thought into where you **NEED** to market, where you **CAN** market affordably, and where you will get the best **RESULTS**.

A **"MARKETING STRATEGY"** looks something like this:

Marketing Strategy
Our marketing strategy emphasizes focus. This is the key. We are a small company with limited resources, so we must focus on certain kinds of products with certain kinds of users. More specifically:

- *We will focus on the 18-24 year old consumers.*
- *We focus on the kind of product quality that produces good word-of-mouth advertising. We must always have a relatively heavy PR component to our marketing, because word-of-mouth is critical.*
- *We are building image and awareness through consistency and distinctiveness in our packaging. The yellow pushpin and red box of the Product X, and the "serious software for serious business" theme, will be repeated consistently throughout our marketing.*
- *We are focusing advertising on several key media which have been proven to reach our target market, as stated above.*

You really have to do this one on your own. The example above is a good strategy for a software company, not yours. You know what market you sell to. What market would be attracted to your product if you had the money for a good marketing campaign? Be sure to mention the words "target", "quality", and "focus". Those are good "catch-phrases" for funding sources.

Write your "Marketing Strategy" on 1 sheet of paper and add it to the pile when you are finished.

For the next section of your Marketing Plan, you need to get out your local phone book, get a copy of the local newspaper, dialup GOOGLE on the Internet and put on your thinking cap. This is where we research what methods are available to market your business and decide which ones are for you.

A sample "Marketing Research" page to guide you:

Marketing Research

Companies Researched:

Daily News, 123 MainStreet, Anytown, US 555-555-1234 Mrs. Smith
Asked about teen age demographics
Total circulation: 50,000 18-24 group 12,000 printed daily
Cost of 8 Column Inch ad: $64.00 per day with contract

Google www.google.com
AdWords campaign for word "widget"
Received 25,000 hits in October 2003
Cost: bid at $.05 per click 1 month =$1250.00

ABC T-Shirts, 456 Main, Anytown, US 555-555-5678 Mr. Jones
T-shirts imprinted with company logo to pass out to teens
Cost: $695.00 for 100 $ 25.00 set-up charge

Outdoor Display, 1456 Main, Anytown, US 555-555-9876 Joe Blow
1 billboard on Main Street for 1 month includes artwork
Cost: $800.00

XYZ Printing 5624 Main, Anytown, US 555-555-0987 Terry King
1000 fliers in 3 colors
Cost: $250.00

WXYZ Radio, 0023 Main, Anytown, US 555-555-8888 Rock Jock
6- 30 second commercials every day for 1 month
Cost: $900.00

This could go on and on. You need at least 5 different types of advertising. The idea is to get actual prices from every type of advertising medium you can think of. Get specifics on any target markets you planned to target in your marketing strategy. You are writing out all of your options for advertising so that you can make a decision as to which will work best for you and how much they will cost. This will take a little time, but it is fun. Tell the people at the different advertisers that you are looking at starting a marketing campaign for your business in the very near future and that it will be an ongoing campaign that will grow over time. They will be very accommodating.

When you have filled a couple of pages with your neatly typed research, place it over on that old pile and get ready to move on.

Now, you have to make some decisions. Here's one big ground rule. Try to keep the entire amount of your funding request UNDER $5000.00. If it HAS to be more, don't go over $7500.00. Why? If you can keep it in that range, you will fit into an even better program of the SBA. The criteria they use to approve a loan are much less stringent. They have historical data that shows them that you have a WHOLE lot better chance of paying back the loan if you keep it in this range, so therefore you are less of a risk. It's NOT a guarantee, but it sure increases your probability of receiving funding almost immediately.

One other thing you have to decide. Are you going to spend the money in one big campaign that takes only a month or are you going to stretch your campaign out over a whole year? That's your decision. If you decide to do it all in one month, then "buy" accordingly knowing that you will have $5000.00 to spend in that month. If you decide to stretch it out over a year, you will have a little over $400.00 a month to spend. A 6-month campaign gives you $800.00 a month...a 3-month campaign gives you $1600.00 a month...YOU gotta decide!

Your "Marketing Budget" should look something like this:

Marketing Budget

Ad Medium	length of time	Cost	Target Market
Google AdWords	1 month	$1250.00	Internet Users
Outdoor Display	1 month	$ 800.00	Drivers, Local
Daily News	45 weeks	$2950.00	12000 teens

Total
$5000.00

After looking at all of the research, I decided to target Internet users because I could reach more of them for less cost. I also wanted to target rush hour drivers on Main Street through the use of a billboard. I also will target teens by placing an ad in the teen section of the Daily News once a week.

Expected Outcome: Since I have done NO advertising of any kind, I fully expect to have a 100% increase in sales after putting my Marketing Plan into action.

That's what it should look like! Let's talk about it for a minute. You'll notice I just have the summary of the Marketing Budget here. What you should do is have a separate sheet for each type of advertising you decide to use. On it, put the company, address, phone and contact person at the top. Then put every detail of the "buy" you plan to make. The cost, the number of ads, the number of Pay-per-clicks, whatever.

The more details, the better!

I also put a justification of why I decided to buy the advertising and what it would do for my market strategy. Don't scrimp on writing here! The lenders want to see that you've done your homework!

How Much Money Will I Make?

The next sheet we need to generate is "Income Projections." This is a section that you REALLY don't want to go CRAZY with! Funding sources see all types of income projections. They laugh out loud out at some of them! These projections are so optimistic that the owner would have to be the world's greatest salesman to come up with those numbers. The proposal is turned down flat! Let's not get our proposal put into that pile, okay?

First, start yourself 3 sheets that look like this:

_____ Percent Projected Increase

Year   Month   Present Sales   Present Profit/Loss
Projected Sales   Projected Profit/Loss

You need to give your projections a little time to get started. For example, if you are writing this in January, make your first month April. That will allow you time to get the money, arrange for the advertising described in your marketing plan and start making sales.

Then, you plug in your historic sales numbers for

April (or a monthly average) along with your historic (or

average) profit/loss. All of this data comes from your

Historical Profit/Loss sheet...the first one you prepared.

Notice the blank at the top of the sheet...
____Percent Projected Increase?

Let's figure a 50% Projected Increase in sales. Your sheet
would look like this:

		Present Sales	Profit/Loss	Proj.Sales	Proj. Profit/Loss
2004	April	$200	($20)	$300.00	$ 80.00
2004	May	$250	$30	$375.00	$155.00

See how that works? You are just taking your

historical data and adding 50% to it.   For this example, I

figured your monthly costs at $220.00 per month. If you

have 0 sales, then project the amount you would receive

from 5 sales that month. The next step is to do the rest of

the calendar year.

The percentages you look at are entirely up to you. Just don't get crazy! If you think you can do a 100% increase, do it…just be prepared to justify it with your marketing plan. This may truly be the case if you haven't been doing much marketing at all.

Whichever percentage you feel the most comfortable with is the one to go with. Look at a bunch of them and pick the one that YOU think YOU can truly do.

What Am I Gonna Do With All Of The Money?

Well, after projecting your income for the next year, as you did in the previous chapter, you know what you're going to make each month. Right? The figures should look a whole lot better than they are now! The next step is to show how that money is going to be spent. Money comes in...some of it has to go back out! This is known as a "Cash Flow Projection"

Funding sources love to see two things:
1. You have a plan for repaying the loan (That's an obvious one!)
2. You have a plan to re-invest in your business (So you won't have to ask for marketing money again!)

Let's assume that your projections showed that your business would generate a profit of $500.00 a month after you started your marketing plan. That's profit over and above what it costs you to run your business. Instead of just putting that into your family checking account, where's what you need to do.

The amount of money your business received from the funding source, in all probability, has to be repaid, with interest.   In your loan request, (coming up in the next chapter), you will ask for a loan term. That's how many years you have to repay the money. And an Interest Rate.

Go to http://www.finaid.org/calculators/loanpayments.phtml and plug in the amount of money you are requesting, the interest rate you are requesting and the number of years. This is usually 5 years, for most sources.   You will get a monthly payment. Write that down.

Let's get back to that $500.00 a month. Say that you requested $3500.00 at 10% interest for 5 years. Your payment would be $74.36, right? So that goes into your cash flow analysis. Let's see, $74.36 divided by $500.00 equals 15% (actually 14.87%). So, 15% of your projected income each month will go to loan repayment.

Let's put another 15% into a marketing fund to buy
more marketing and get more profits. And finally, let's put
another 15% into a "rainy day" fund for business
emergencies. That still leaves you, the business owner 55%,
or $275.00, in your pocket.

You need to show that like this:

Projected Monthly Profit	$500.00
Loan Repayment	$ 75.00
Marketing Fund	$ 75.00
Emergency Fund	$ 75.00
Owner Profit	$275.00

You need to do one of these for every month of the
calendar year. The monthly profit figures will be different,
as will be the marketing fund and emergency fund figures.
The percentages for these will remain constant each month,
but the actual dollar amounts will change since the profits
change each month.

It should look something like this when you are

done:

	April Total	May	June
Projected Monthly Profit **$4500.00**	$500.00	$550.00	$400.00
Loan Repayment .... **$ 675.00**	$ 75.00	$ 75.00	$ 75.00
Marketing Fund .... **$ 675.00**	$ 75.00	$ 82.50	$ 60.00
Emergency Fund .... **$ 675.00**	$ 75.00	$ 82.50	$ 60.00
Owner Profit **$2475.00**	$275.00	$310.00	$205.00

You get the idea. Over at the right side, total all of

the rows up for the calendar year. Your figures are going

to be different; this is just an example.

What does this sheet of paper do for you? It lets the funding source know two things. You have made plans to repay the loan and have the money to do so. You have also reinvested in your business by setting aside more marketing money as well as an emergency fund. The emergency fund is important because the funding sources will see it as a way to make the loan repayment even if you have a terrible month. That is good business management. That's what the lenders like to see.

Please don't think that this is only going to happen on paper. You really need to set up these two accounts. Actually 2 different checking accounts or savings accounts. It is vital to pay your business before you pay yourself, if you want the business to prosper and grow.

Well, that's all of the hard stuff! The rest is just wrapping it up and putting a pretty bow on it before we give it to the funding sources. That wasn't so bad, was it? You've learned a lot about your business. The whole process should make you feel like more of a business owner, more in control of your business and its money. It should feel pretty good to you!

Let's wrap this thing up and get to the fun part. Good job so far!

Chapter Thirteen
Wrapping It All Up

First of all, go back and dig out the first sheet, your

" Executive Summary".

Now, you can finally write your own. Take a look at the

example on pages 8 and 9 and write your own. You have

all of the information and have made all of the decisions

needed to write a great one. Go ahead, I'll wait!

Now, let's get everything in the proper order.

1. Executive Summary
2. Company Summary
3. Management Summary
4. Products/Services
5. Market Analysis Worksheet
6. Market Analysis Paragraphs
7. Historical Sales Data
8. Sales Goals
9. Marketing Strategy
10. Marketing Research
11. Marketing Plan
12. Marketing Budget
13. Income Projections
14. Cash Flow Projections
15. Loan Proposal (Next Chapter)

See how that allows for a smooth flow of information? From understanding you and your company to seeing your historical data to seeing your marketing plan, it all makes sense!

**Here's How Much Money I'm Gonna Need
And Why You Should Loan It To Me.**

Okay, let's recap. You have made:

1. A business synopsis
2. A historical profit/loss statement
3. A marketing plan
4. An income projection for 1 calendar year
5. A cash flow analysis

In anyone's book, that's a business plan! Now we need to write a loan request. This is a simple, one page letter saying the following:

1. I am requesting a $ _____ business loan for marketing funds in order to make my business profitable.

2. I am requesting the loan for a term of 5 years at an interest rate at or below 10%

3. I am submitting a business plan to justify this request.

4. I would like an appointment to discuss this request at your earliest convenience.

5. If you have any questions about this information, contact me at:

You need to put this in your own words, in language that you are comfortable using. Don't make it sound too business-like. Don't try to sound like a lawyer. (unless you are!) Don't try to sound like you do this all of the time (unless you do!). Try to sound like an ordinary person who is passionate about their business, knows it will succeed and just needs some financial assistance.

Now, make about 10 copies of each part of your business plan. Get 10 decent binders, (not REAL fancy) and make yourself 10 business plan portfolios.

Pat yourself on the back; you've done something that very few people ever have! You should feel proud of your accomplishment!

Where Do I Go? Who Do I See?

First of all, leave your tidy pile of loan proposals at home on the dining room table or somewhere...you don't need them at this point. Your next step is to enter the wonderful world of banking. Don't shudder like that! It really isn't that bad!

Go to your bank...the one you have a checking account /savings account/Christmas club with and ask for a BUSINESS LOAN APPLICATION. You will probably get referred to a loan officer of the bank. He/She will more than likely ask you what you need the loan for.

Just reply, "I'm exploring funding options for a loan for my business." DON'T SAY TOO MUCH MORE THAN THAT! THIS IS NOT THE TIME TO DISCUSS YOUR PROPOSAL! Just get the application form, the loan officers' name or card, thank them politely and leave.

Repeat this at 2 other banks in your area.

Bring the applications home and start to fill them out. One of the first things you will run into is that they ask for a tax I.D. number or your E.I.N. . If you have a tax number from your state, of course, enter it. You probably don't have an E.I.N. unless you have employees.

The next thing everyone is intimidated by is the collateral list. Fill it out! This doesn't mean that you will be pledging it all to get the money. You have to realize that ALL funding sources want some sort of collateral for funds that they loan you, in case you don't pay them back. You are asking for $5000.00 or less! Categories like household furniture, computer equipment, electronics will fill the collateral columns well. If you own, or are buying, a home, list it also. It proves that you are able to take on a BIG debt and make the payments on a timely basis.

Your payment on $5000.00 at 10% for 5 years will be under $110.00 a month. If you haven't convinced yourself, through all of the work you've done on your business plan, that you can make more than that each month, you need to stop this process now. If you don't believe it, how can a funding source?

Fill out all 3 applications as completely as possible. Put the application and one of your business plan packages in a manila envelope and send it to the bank to the attention of the loan officer you got the application from. DON'T TAKE IT IN PERSON! Mark down the date that you sent the packages and call the loan officers exactly 1 week later.

All you want to accomplish with your phone call is to see if they have had a chance to review your application and business plan AND make an appointment with them to discuss it.

Call all three loan officers and set up appointments. If they just say that their bank doesn't do loans of that sort, or anything that turns you down immediately…just smile, thank them and ask them to send you a letter to that effect. (They have to, by Federal Law.)

At this point, I have to let you in on a little secret. You probably don't want to get your funding through the bank anyway! The Small Business Administration is where you really want to go. However, you have to prove to the SBA that you are not able to get funding from any other banking sources. These rejection letters are EXACTLY what you need!

If you do get appointments with your banks, take them seriously. The odds are that you will be rejected by them anyway, so don't get real nervous about it. The experience of having someone that deals with financial matters everyday go over your business plan will be invaluable. Listen to them, let them view you as a business person, it will help your attitude toward your business immensely.

After all, most loan officers will be impressed by the work you have done on your business plan, the research and planning put into it. They will view you as someone who is serious about their business. A friend at the local banks is never a bad thing for anyone!

So, 3 banks have turned you down. That's a good thing! It's time to move on to the next step.

The Next Step

Okay, you've done a lot of work on your business. You've taken a hard look at your costs; you've come up with a marketing plan; you've been rejected by traditional lending sources. It's time to go to the source that is waiting there to help you.

Go to:

http://www.sba.gov/financing/microparticipants.html and find the SBA Intermediary in your area. Most of them have certain counties they work with in your state. Almost every state has one organization that works statewide if your county is not covered. Send copies of your rejection letters, a copy of your business plan and a cover letter requesting assistance in obtaining a MICROLOAN to the Intermediary. Follow up with them in 1 week by phone.

****

If you do not live in the United States, check out this funding source search engine. Just type in your country, leave the other two boxes blank.

http://www.microcreditsummit.org/forms/database.htm

The United States Embassy in every country has information and assistance in acquiring microloan funding. The embassies are generally located in major cities. A listing of US Embassies can be found here:

http://www.usembassy.state.gov .

The process for microloans will vary from country to country, but all of the funding sources will require some, or all, of what we have prepared throughout this book.

****
*

The SBA Intermediary will guide you through the process rather painlessly. They will try to sign you up for a lot of business knowledge kind of courses for free. Some of them are very good…some are a waste of time. Take what you feel you need…they are FREE! Just don't get sidetracked and forget about your business all together.

With everything that you have already done on your business plan, the SBA process should take very little time…7-10 days. Once the SBA approves you, you are referred to a bank in your area, (maybe one of the banks that rejected you!), to handle your loan. The SBA will guarantee your loan to the bank. You will actually be borrowing money from the bank, but at lower rates and the repayment is guaranteed by the U.S. government.

Sealing The Deal

Here are a few things to put in your cover letter to the SBA that will help assure your acceptance.

Make it very clear to the SBA if you are:
Disabled,
A Minority,
A Woman,
A Veteran.
This will make a big difference in your acceptance.

Make a statement to the effect that you are willing for the bank to cut checks to your advertising sources directly. That way they know that the money is going directly to where you said it would. This increases their trust and gives them more control over the process. Just write something like this: *If you think it is necessary, I am willing to allow the lender to pay all advertising vendors directly, thereby assuring that the loan funds are used as stated.*

Be willing to accept some business training from the SBA, especially if it is offered on-line. As I cautioned before, The SBA tends to train you to death if you let them, so be cautious. Training is great; just don't ignore your business entirely.

Be business-like in all of your dealings with SBA. Ask questions about things you don't understand. They love that! But, don't waste their time by missing appointments to call or visit their office. Use email as much as possible. Just show them a little respect and they will react very favorably.

For our world friends, these same rules will apply. The customs and processes may be different, but the same things about any disability, minority, gender, etc. will be the same. The respect shown to people who are trying to help you applies throughout the world.

You may be asked to change your business plan around a bit, or add to it. What we have put together here is a basic plan; they may want more or less. Work with them; make it a learning experience. It will do nothing but improve your business knowledge and help make your business more profitable.

References and Other Stuff

http://www.sba.gov

http://www.cyberatlas.com

http://www.microcreditsummit.org/forms/database.htm

http://www.usembassy.state.gov

http://www.sba.gov/financing/microparticipants.html

My email address: dennislively@gmail.com

My website: http://www.DennisLively.com

An Example Loan Proposal

The following is a basic business plan and loan proposal I have prepared as an example for you to work with. It is not as detailed as yours should be, but the form should be the same.

Business Synopsis

My name is Dennis Lively and I am the owner of LiveMark Web. My company sells Internet Access to consumers. In this area there are 5 other Internet Access Providers. The market for Internet Access has grown an average of 5% each year for the last 3 years. There are 7618 Internet users in our county. 381 new users, on average, are available each year. 610 present users switched services last year.

My Internet Access Service is faster, more full-featured and less expensive than any of my competitors. I also am the only provider to offer free customer service, 24 hours a day, year-round.

I have 28 years of experience in business management and 10 years experience on the Internet. I have lived in this area for 10 years.

This needs to be longer and more detailed. Put in some more details about your competition…their prices, their weaknesses and strengths, that sort of thing. Also add some more about the features of your product that make it different from your competition. Any experience you have should be highlighted as well.

Historical Profit/Loss Statement

Year	Month	Sales	Costs	Profit/Loss
2003	January	100.00	220.00	(120.00)
2003	February	180.00	220.00	(40.00)
2003	March	280.00	220.00	60.00
2003	April	220.00	220.00	-0-
2003	May	300.00	220.00	80.00
2003	June	200.00	220.00	(20.00)
2003	July	240.00	220.00	20.00
2003	August	250.00	220.00	30.00
2003	September	350.00	220.00	130.00
2003	October	200.00	220.00	(20.00)
2003	November	220.00	220.00	-0-
2003	December	350.00	220.00	130.00
Totals		2890.00	2640.00	250.00

Cost Schedule

Internet Service (1/2 of bill)	*$10.00*
Domain Name ($8.00 per year)	*$ 1.00*
Web Hosting	*$ 9.00*
Wholesaler Fee	*$25.00*
Cost of materials	*$75.00*
Marketing	*$10.00*
Shipping	*$10.00*
Mortgage (10% of bill)	*$50.00*
Utilities (10% of bill)	*$20.00*
Insurance (10% of bill)	*$10.00*
Total	*$220.00*

These fixed costs were figured from actual invoices or contracts. The percentage of household bills is figured upon $250.00 per month average business income versus $2500. 00 per month employment income (10%)

Of course, your figures will be different. This is the form the cost schedule needs to be in. Explain how you come up with the figures. True invoices, contracts, etc. Tell them how you arrive at the percentage of household expenses.

Marketing Plan and Budget

I plan to buy the following advertising:
Newspaper Ads:
Daily Bugle 8 Column Inches a week for 52 weeks $2496.00
Trader Weekly 8 Column Inches a week for 52 weeks$604.00

Internet Ads:
Google PayPerClick Ads$40.00/month for 10 months
$ 400.00

Radio Ads:
WXYZ 1500, 30 sec spots over a 5 month period $1500.00
Total Marketing Budget $5000.00

Daily Bugle	*Trader Weekly*	*Google*
123 Main	*456 Market*	*200 Main*
Any Town	*Any Town*	*Any Town*
555-555-1111	*555-555-1111*	*555-555-1111*
Attn: Joe Blow	*John Doe*	*Jane Doe*
Circulation		
50,000 daily	*30,000 weekly*	*10,000,000 daily*

Of course, your information will be different. The important thing is to write down accurate costs and the amount of advertising you are getting for your money. The advertisers will give you their circulation figures if you ask. Always ask for them. They help to prove your point. Try to make the advertising as targeted as possible without spending over $5000.00 on the entire plan.

You might preface the marketing plan with the following statement:

After looking at my business profit/loss statement, I have conceived the following market plan. This plan, if enacted, will generate at least a 100% increase in sales, based on the demographics of the advertisers and the fact that we did NO advertising in 2003.

Income Projections

2003 Year	2003 Month	2003 Sales	Proj. Costs	Proj. Profit/Loss	Proj. Costs	Profit/Loss
2004	January	100.00	220.00	(120.00)	200.00	220.00 (20.00)
2004	February	180.00	220.00	(40.00)	360.00	220.00 140.00
2004	March	280.00	220.00	60.00	560.00	220.00 340.00
2004	April	220.00	220.00	-0-	440.00	220.00 220.00
2004	May	300.00	220.00	80.00	600.00	220.00 380.00
2004	June	200.00	220.00	(20.00)	400.00	220.00 180.00
2004	July	240.00	220.00	20.00	480.00	220.00 260.00
2004	August	250.00	220.00	30.00	500.00	220.00 280.00
2 004	September	350.00	220.00	130.00	700.00	220.00 480.00
2004	October	200.00	220.00	(20.00)	400.00	220.00 180.00
2004	November	220.00	220.00	-0-	440.00	220.00 220.00
2004	December	350.00	220.00	130.00	700.00	220.00 480.00
Totals		2890.00	2640.00	250.00	5780.00	2640.00 3140.00

Looks a LOT better now, right? You still have to take your loan repayment, marketing fund and emergency fund amounts out of it in your cash flow analysis sheet. That's next.

Cash Flow Analysis

Loan Repayment ($100.00/Month)
Marketing Fund (20% of remainder)
Emergency Fund (same as marketing fund)

Year	Month	Gross Profit Net	Loan	Marketing	Emergency
2004	February	140.00 / 24.00	100.00	8.00	8.00
2004	March	340.00 / 144.00	100.00	48.00	48.00
2004	April	220.00 / 72.00	100.00	24.00	24.00
2004	May	380.00 / 168.00	100.00	56.00	56.00
2004	June	180.00 / 48.00	100.00	16.00	16.00
2004	July	260.00 / 96.00	100.00	32.00	32.00
2004	August	280.00 / 108.00	100.00	36.00	36.00
2 004	September	480.00 / 228.00	100.00	76.00	76.00
2004	October	180.00 / 48.00	100.00	16.00	16.00
2004	November	220.00 / 72.00	100.00	24.00	24.00
2004	December	480.00 / 228.00	100.00	76.00	76.00
Total		3160.00 / 1236.00	1100.00	412.00	412.00

As you can see, my marketing plan will generate enough additional revenue to, not only pay for the cost of the loan, but also allow me to set aside money for marketing and emergencies. It also greatly increases my net profit.

That's really about it! You just need to make sure your figures all add up and are in neat little columns. You are giving this proposal to number-crunchers, after all!

Just write yourself a cover letter that says something like:

> *Enclosed, you will find a copy of my loan proposal and my business plan to support my loan request.*
> *The process of preparing this data has made me more aware of my business and forced me to plan it out much better.*
> *I appreciate your time and effort in reviewing these documents and look forward to hearing from you soon regarding your decision. I will contact you on (DATE) to follow up with you. If you have any questions in the meantime, please contact me at 555-555-1111.*

Sincerely,
Joe Blow, Owner
Gizmos, Inc.

The End?

NO! This isn't the end. It should be a beginning for you. You have a much better understanding of YOUR business. You have a much better plan to grow your business. That plan is not set in stone. It will change as your business changes. It's a good idea to take a look at your profit/loss every month. It's a good idea to take a look at your marketing plan every quarter. Change it as needed to keep your profit/loss on the positive side.

THE MOST IMPORTANT THING YOU CAN DO IS TO WRITE DOWN YOUR GOALS FOR YOUR BUSINESS AND YOUR GOALS FOR YOURSELF. THEY ARE NOT THE SAME! YOUR BUSINESS MAY HELP YOUR PERSONAL GOALS, BUT THEY ARE NOT THE SAME.

THERE IS SOMETHING MAGICAL IN WRITING DOWN GOALS AND PLANS. I KNOW IT SOUNDS GOOFY, BUT IT IS TRUE. YOU'VE STARTED THAT PROCESS BY WRITING YOUR BUSINESS PLAN, NOW WRITE DOWN SOME GOALS FOR YOUR BUSINESS IN MEASURABLE TERMS...*I WILL BE MAKING A $500 A MONTH PROFIT IN MY BUSINESS BY APRIL 1 2004.*

THEN WRITE A PLAN TO ACHIEVE THAT GOAL...EXACTLY LIKE YOUR MARKETING PLAN YOU JUST DID!

You've accomplished a lot! I'm proud that you have gone through the process. 95% of the people who want to get into business NEVER do this and many of them fail. You've taken some of the right steps to success.

I wish you great success in all that you want in life. Thank you for being a reader.

Dennis Lively
October 2003

www.ingramcontent.com/pod-product-compliance
Lightning Source LLC
Chambersburg PA
CBHW051343170526
45166CB00002B/934